The Human Zoo

A Death Row Poetry Collection

Compiled and Edited
by Timothy Moxley

Poundstone Press
Seattle Washington

Published by
Poundstone Press
1122 E. Pike Street
Seattle, Washington 98122

www·humanzoo·com

Copyright C 1997 by Timothy Moxley

All rights reserved. No part of this book may be reproduced or transmitted in any form or by any means without the written permission of the Publisher, except where permitted by law.

Library of Congress Cataloging in Pub. Data
Moxley, Timothy.
    The Human Zoo/ by Timothy Moxley
        p.   cm
    ISBN 0-9660602-1-0
    I. Title.
    97-92556   CIP
Manufactured in the United States of America

First Edition

I would like to thank all the Public Information Officers and their staff for providing me with the necessary data to complete this project. Thanks also to Paul for his advice and guidance and especially to Julie for her love, patience & editing, to Tom for his indominable spirit and finally to my mom for teaching me the meaning of hope; I couldn't have done it without you.

Grateful acknowledgment is made to:
Harvard University Press.
Poem #1716, is reprinted with permission of the publishers and the Trustees of Amherst College from, The Poems of Emily Dickinson, Thomas H. Johnson, ed., Cambridge, Mass,: The Belknap Press of Harvard University Press, Copyright C 1951, 1955, 1979, 1983 by the President and Fellows of Harvard College.

Dedicated to truth, justice and
the American way.

Death is like the insect
Menacing the tree,
Competent to kill it,
But decoyed may be.

Bait it with the balsam,
Seek it with the knife,
Baffle, if it cost you
Everything in life.

Then, if it have burrowed
Out of reach of skill,
Ring the tree and leave it,-
'Tis the vermin's will.

-Emily Dickinson

Introduction

This book is a collection of poems written by death row inmates from all over the United States. Format limits made it necessary to occasionally break a line or add punctuation and I did correct some spelling errors for clarity, but the words are their own.

Although it was my idea to make this book it would not have happened if the inmates didn't agree to share their poems and experiences with young people who are today facing many of the same problems they struggled with 10 or 20 years ago. During my correspondence with the men & women who live on the row I learned some very interesting things about them, about myself and the society in which we live.For example, many of the people now facing capital punishment were repeat offenders as adults, but before they entered the adult prison system a surprising number were juvenile offenders first !

A 56 year old man who has been on death row for 15 years in Pennsylvania wrote, "It all started from going into my fathers pockets or my mothers purse and taking some change. That road of what you might call innocent taking was the same road that led to death row."Another inmate wrote, "Let me assure you that you don't have to be guilty of committing a crime for the state to prosecute you. All you need's a bad reputation such as I had and if a crime goes down in your neighborhood and the cops have your number, you can bet your boots they'll be on your doorstep asking you about the crime."

An inmate in Arizona wrote, "When i was younger i thought i was sly and the law would never catch me. I started using drugs at about 15 and at about 16 drugs started using me if you read this letter to the kids tell them to stay away from drugs, gangs, and illegal activities or they will surely end up in prison & from someone who is in prison i can tell you it is no place to be." Many inmates admitted they knew it was wrong to hurt people - to rape, steal or kill, but they blamed any thing that happened at the time on everything but themselves. They never took responsibility for their actions. Until finally, in the isolation of their cells on the row some people have faced the truth. Some don't ever make it that far. "Six or ten or fifteen years without a letter from home, no phone calls and no visitors, it wears you down," one guy wrote, "tough don't mean nothing cause its you against the system. If they don't beat you, other inmates might, or they rape you or stab you for lookin' at they boyfriend. It ain't hell it's worse."

Another guy wrote, "Every day I wake up in this hell I'm glad to be one day closer to dien." Their words of caution and warning are endless.

Some are more subtle but no less powerful. One of the few women to respond to my request wrote, "Tell them for me to stop & take a look at what they got then think about what they'll lose." During the three years I spent putting this book together people often asked me why I was doing it and what I hoped to accomplish.

First, I want to improve communication between youth-at-risk and educators. We have a basic responsibility to each other as human beings, from our parents to the grocer down the street and we're all connected by the air that we breath and the water drink. As such we must share the burdens of society, not be a burden. Communication is just one of the ways we can carry, or create a burden as individuals and strong writing skills help us explain our ideas and actions more clearly.

Poetry can be an artistic and powerful method of communication. The words we say reveal some of our feelings, but it is often the unspoken word that holds the most truth, or hides it. Sometimes we don't speak up because we are afraid of being wrong, or make noise to confuse the listener. In fact, one of the most important parts of communication is listening. Only when we truly listen can we understand and respond intelligently.

The second thing I want to accomplish is to break the cycle of violence by taking something from the very end of the cycle; poetry from death row inmates, then show it to young people who are just now starting to get into trouble at school with drugs, their parents or the law. Actions may speak louder than words, but violence is no substitute for conversation and writing is one of the most constructive forms of communication we have. By writing our ideas down we can preserve them and remember or share them, but writing also lets us review what we say and how we say it. That's important if we want people to take us seriously and respect us. The writers in this collection made the effort to write and respond to my request for poetry. I asked them one question:

"if you write poetry, would you be willing to contribute a poem or two to this collection to help young people see the danger of starting off life by going down the wrong road?" The right path isn't easy to find & can be harder to stick to once you stray, but after reading this book I think you'll agree the hard road just brings heartache and sadness to everyone involved. Prison is no place to grow up and it sure as hell is no place to die. This poetry is the result of countless years of pain & suffering for the victims, their families and the inmates themselves. We can't change the past but we can change the future, and education, not incarceration is the key. I ask you to read these poems and think about the people who did not, or will not, live to realize their full potential. Your future is in your hands. Education is the key to your future & this book is a door. Open it and read these poems from people who have just one thing left to offer. They are the voices from the deep end of the tunnel.
Listen carefully.

The Human Zoo

Table of Contents

Broken Dreams..................................16
Empty Silence...................................18
House of Steel and Stone...................19
Waiting ...waiting............................22
A Walk In My Life............................26
Take a Trip.......................................27
Goodbye.. 29
Ten Bad Men................................... 32
In Prison..34
Death Row Dialog............................36
Forked Tongue.................................37
To Row or Not To Row....................39
Politics of Death..............................42
Dust and Ruin.................................44
Innocent..46
Justice is a Crime............................47
This Smile is Just for You................50
Lost Family 51
Death's Stare.................................. 54
It's Not Too Late for You.................58
no title...62
Prison is..64
Finality..66
The Cell...67
Mail...68

Empty	69
My Friend	70
On the Inside	71
Prison is A Pit	74
A Facade of Happiness	76
A Lonely Look Out the Window	77
Touching a Life	78
Remember Me	80
In Jail with the Lord	81
Faith	82
What is My Name	84
A Night in Prison	86
A Letter to God	88
Todays Never End	92
Time in the Bricks	94
Judgement Day	96
Freedom	100
I Search	101
The Cycle	102
Another Mountain	103
Long Narrow Trail	104
What the Clouds See	105
Brothers of the Clan	106
untitled	108
untitled #2	109
untitled #3	110
In Bondage	112

The Human Zoo

contents continued

Innocent Cries
from the Shadows..................113
The Tomb 116
Tears of Sorrow/Hell..............118
Hear My Words.....................119
I Never Thought....................122
Prison 126
Johnny Got a Gun 128
A Ticket to Hell....................130
The Dream Makers Wall.........132
Prisoners of Color.................136
Utu.....................................137
Mindfield.............................139*
Epilogue..............................142

*Note editor's poem

Anonymous

D.O.B. 7/20/61.   Date sentenced 10/28/83.

I never realized why I did what I did to end up in jail when I was a teenager. Kids get smarter quicker today, but still don't have the common sense to use that knowledge for positive things. It helps to set the inner self into a solid meaning so that the academic knowledge can be used positively and not lost in the confusion of what we go though in our daily lives.

Broken Dreams

All the lonely faces
that were looking for success
never finding stardom,
failing in their quest.
Boulevards across the nations
are known for such as these,
they appear from everywhere
with big hopes, wishes and dreams.
Most run out of money
before they find their rightful place,
then before they know it
they're caught in the city's rat race.
Some only want to go home, they're
afraid what their family might say
They went out looking for the top,
now they're left in total dismay.
Most end up in Prostitution
hustling for their next meal,
others start selling drugs,
some begin to rob and steal.
This is Hollywood,
a teenager's scene
looking for the stars and
only finding broken dreams.

Anonymous is on death row in America.

Edward Bennett

D.O.B ?/?/69.   Date sentenced 10/18/88.

No additional information was provided by this inmate.

Disparaging in heart and mind for all the dreams now gone. Gone, gone by my own hand and helpless to ever retreive them.

Empty Silence

Voices calling out to one another
Mindless words spoken in desperation
Used to fill the empty space.
Souls abandoned after damning scrutiny
Left in mortal silence to twist and writhe.
Voices calling out to fill ones own ear
That one voice is at least real. Claustrophobia
spirits not able to roam"No flowers for this
grave" reads the epitaph on the stone.
It's an empty grave, filled with No One. But
No One was a special person. He had
thoughts ideas, and deep feelings Had a voice
that wanted to sing. But the beautiful song
was silenced into a scream, and No One
called out to Anybody Even if it was in anger.
At least Anybody listened to his plea
But then Anybody was a special person too.
And was the sounding-board any time
No One called out. Then one day, Some One
called out to No One -emptiness, no one
responded so Some One called to No One
again, still empty silence. Then Some Body
told Some One that No One was executed
during the night. Some One started to cry
in the empty silence.

House of Steel and Stone

As I grew up, I lived six miles from a cage.
A penitentiary, a house of steel and stone.
Not once did I ever look to see, or care to know
the depths of harsh reality, grinding on those men's
souls. My brash little mind filled with rage insisting
to live life my way.
40's, 5th's, kegs's, the dope biz, Coke, Smack, LSD trips.
Gangs, a power trip, hatred, rush of violence- I loved it.
It's a guaranteed critical burnout, I reached terminal
velocity.
Armed robbery, bullets flying, one went down, another
one dead with a cap to their head.
So now I sit entombed, in a house of steel and stone.
Not just seeing it with my eyes, but feeling its coldness in
my soul. It's harsh it's real it's a brutal place a place filled
with tears. The years stretch out indeterminately, time
filled with anxiety. I awake with raw grinding depression
inside this concrete box, confused. Confused with the
dreadful frustration of having to face another day.
Another day of routine boredom, aggravation, anger and
petty hate.
Hate now of self as I lay awake through the miserable
night. Nights of tossing and turning with loss, loneliness
and despair. Disparaging in heart and mind for all the
dreams now gone. Gone, gone by my own hand and
helpless to ever retrieve them. They ache, ache with
regret and remorse, a sorrow living of its own.

It's a life for no one.
No one wants it. It destroys body, mind and
soul. The soul struggling for something
positive to feel...
The mind having to fight for survival is
something very real... The body starving for
vitality yet dying from isolation's atrophy...
to want out of this living grave.
But unlike me you can look within---
and end the nightmare before it begins.

Truly life is yours to live
but live it with love, peace, hopes and dreams.
Understanding one thing, and this you'd better
know
God can not be mocked;
You will reap what you sow.

So now it's up to you, even though...
I cannot correctly reveal the truth of the
crushing weight of a life in the penitentiary.
Or how one deals
with the terrible hurt and woe
within this house of steel and stone.

Ed Bennett is on death row in Nevada.

Clifford Boggess

D.O.B. 6/11/65.   Date sentenced 10/27/86.

I am a born-again christian now, a man who fully admits my guilt and wants to do whatever I can to make things right during the time I have left on this earth.

And on and on it endlessly goes
year after never ending year.

Waiting... Waiting

Few people, will ever understand the pain and
suffering endured by a man trapped within the
bowels of the Texas-Death-Machine;

A modern day dungeon whose stench of death
Is the same as that ancient putrid stench has
been for thousands upon thousands of years
In countless millions of lives.

It tries to suffocate you and drown you
Until every breath of every day and night
Is but a desperate agonizing gasp;
One more meager and pathetic attempt
To remain afloat in the nauseous cesspool
We call Life.

If it would but set you free
Or mercifully, thankfully, kill you
It would be more welcome and humane
Than the slow and agonizing torture
of endless oppression and misery,

It's tools are hidden, yet everywhere
Not easily recognized, yet known.
A water-torture of thoughts and attitudes

Voiced hatreds, misunderstanding and ignorance;
Restraints of Writs & Court Orders
Knives of Indictments & Death Warrants.
Harmless paper, yet just as deadly
As any word ever spoken
By Casear, Herod, Attila, Hitler
And on and on it endlessly goes
Year after never-ending year.
A mega-ton weight upon your back
You are continually broken, pressed down
Wondering how much longer you can live
With such mind-shattering pain.
Waiting and hoping and waiting
To finally be crushed completely
To disappear into restful oblivion.
Waiting... waiting...
Mouthing silent screams;
Waiting... waiting...
And still you live on.
Waiting and waiting...
Tick-tock... waiting... Tick-tock...
Time passing slowly over you
A chainsaw shredding now bloodied
human flesh. Tick-tock... tick-tock...
Waiting... hoping... waiting
For the end that never comes.
Tick-tock...waiting... tick-tock... waiting
Waiting...waiting... waiting... waiting...

Clifford Boggess is on death row in Texas.

Jeffery Doughtie

D.O.B. 10/03/61. Date sentenced 6/10/94

I sent along some things for you to read to the kids and maybe hearing it straight from someone who is waiting to die for not listening will perk them up some.

What's ahead for me is without any question, everlasting life, with Jesus in Heaven.

A Walk in My Life

As I sit in this lonely cell
thinking back on a life of hell,
drunken day's and drug filled nights
all alone and out of sight.
My mind goes back to the constant pain
never wanted, shuffled and changed.
Home to home to home, and state to state
unloved and abused, I learned such hate.
For a few short years I knew such joy
a loving wife and a baby boy.
I learned of Christ, and oh what laughter
before I knew it, I had a daughter.
Then out of my past, like a thief in the night
rose the demons of drugs in my win-less fight.
I hung my head and stared at my feet
because in my heart I knew I'd been beat.

And now as I sit here on Death Row
There are some things I've come to know.
Life is sweet and freedom is dear
the path is long, but the way is clear.
Never give up and fight to the end
to lay down and die would be such a sin.
Straight ahead and up life's pass
ever onward until the very last.

Take A Trip

You can go now where I'm going
or you can stay right where I've been.
In a world filled with pain
loneliness and sin.

You see my life is over
but friends have shown me the way.
So before I leave this cold, gray earth
there's some things I'd like to say.

I've lived the life and played the games
drunk and drugged till I didn't know my name.
Glamorous? Yeah, I guess you could call it that
living on the sidewalk, stretched flat on my back.

For days on end I'd walk the street
no food in my belly, or even shoes on my feet.
I robbed and stole, I took human life
never caring a damn, in a world filled with strife.

And then one day I got this call
and no it never came from any phone on a wall.
It came from God, and was placed from within
He said, "Turn away from your life of sin."

Now freedom is cheap, but it sure ain't free
because I had to face the monster I had
come to be.
But thanks to friends and my God up above
who shared with me his wisdom and love.
Am I free? Even though in jail?
I say yes, because I'm free from hell.
Am I free? Yes I'd say so
I was set free from here on Death Row.

So you can Listen now
or you can Learn it then.
The drink, the drugs, the girls, the sin
It's the devil's game and you can never win.
It all comes down to what you want to be.
Either in here, or out there
Only through Christ can you ever be free.

Goodbye

Goodbye is always hard to say
Especially to an old dear friend
It seems like only yesterday
That our earthly walk began.

We faced lifes troubles
Each daily ounce of pain.
And whenever I would slip and fall
You would pick me up again.

We both made promises we knew
we couldn't keep.
Because in every life there are victories
but also there are defeats.

I hope and pray you can understand
what it is I'm about to say.
To feel no guilt, no pain, no remorse
for my decision to go away.

Think not of death as I'm strapped
on that gurney
Only of life and my
wonderful journey.

What's ahead for me is without
any question, Everlasting life
with Jesus in Heaven.

To feel sorry for me, I should certainly
hope not!
Because without his promise
just what have you got?

You walk this earth day after day
empty of spirit, lost and alone.
Only through Christ,
can you ever find home.

So smile for me
and say your goodbye
keep your head held high
and try not to cry.

To do any less would be such a shame
To doubt the Faith I put in his name.

Jeffery Doughtie is on death row in Texas.

Tim Dunlap

D.O.B. 9/22/68. Date sentenced 4/20/92.

I am on Death Row in Idaho and I have a death sentence in Ohio. I've enclosed a poem which I wrote.

... the executioner was having fun
threw two to the lions,
now there's but one...

Ten Bad Men

Ten bad men standing in a line
a shot was fired now there are nine
Nine bad men the forces were great
one man explodes
changes the number to eight
Eight bad men to settle the score
but the guillotine slices all the way to four
Four bad men wanting to be free
but the cyanide gas
puts it to three
Three bad men
the executioner was having fun
threw two to the lions
now there's but one
One bad man climbed the fence to run
but an ax was thrown in fury
now there are none
No bad men
what is there to say
what is there to do
what would you say
If the bad man were you.

Tim Dunlap is on death row in Idaho.

Priscilla Ford

D.O.B. 2/10/29.   Date sentenced 4/29/82.

Tell the young people that education is the beforehand answer. Something for nothing conditions are not worth the time served. "In Prison" tells about those doomed. It is a terrible fate.

Where can you get three meals a day ?
You're kept alive and don't have to pay
In prison.

In Prison

Where can you get three meals a day?
You're kept alive and don't have to pay
In prison

Where can you get your laundry done?
While you shoot the breeze and have
your fun
In prison

Where can you get a bed to sleep in ?
a room of your own - stool and wash basin
In prison
You get medication and physician's advice
and make good friends both naughty
and nice
In prison
Where can you get either a dump or parole?
by a board of police whose job promotion
is goal In prison
You get to hear radio or watch TV
and you won't pay a penny for electricity
In prison.

Priscilla Ford is on death row in Nevada.

Donald Hall

D.O.B. 8/11/46. Date sentenced 6/18/87.

Continuing to deny or find excuses for errant behavior only serves as a means of justification to return to it:It's not mom pop, family or community it's you, man! You've got a mind,use it...for a better life.

It was a choice I should have made
to mend my life and change my ways.

Death Row Dialog

What's up killer, what's it gon' be
I'll beg your pardon, are you talking to me?
Take a look around, who else you see?
It can't be me, I ain't killed no-body.

That's the rapp that's going around
that all the killers are puttin' down
been falsly accused, the jury was confused
put me in jail where I'm bein' abused
Violatin' my rights, can't you see
I don't deserve the death penalty.

But what about yo' victim that you
executed with yo' own death penalty
that you instituted?

That's just my point and I'm going
to pursue it. I've been tried and convicted
but I just didn't do it.
Not guilty, not guilty to the end will I be
I guess no one deserves it but little old me
If not for this then surely for that
for my record to date goes way back
It doesn't matter you how this turns out
for me cause by the spirit of truth
I'm free, free, free!

Forked Tongue

You tell me you have faith in God
But when tested by the devil
Your tongue reveals another mind
It drops to another level

You speak of truth but practice lies
So when I hear yur words
I seperate them from your fleshy hide
Because your actions are absurd

It's hard to take the word of one
Who does not practice what he preaches
Or one who fails to even try
To apply the things that he teaches

A different face for every man
Which one is for real?
Whoever hosts your company
To him your tongue appeals

When you're in the host of those
Who speak of Godly things
Your tongue is as an angles wisp
such pleasant words it brings
But when you're hosting crime and vice
Your tongue splits as though twice

The words it spews spells how confused
Your mind and spirit's plight
Christian, Muslim, Buddhist Monk
Whatever you say you are
Rights and traditions with out faith and
devotion won't get you very far

I'd rather see you act, Than hear you
any day, I'd rather have you show me
Than merely speak the way
My sights a better student
and more observant then my ear
words sometimes confuse
What I see is mostly clear
I don't want to hear about your caddy
Or all the dope you sold
Or about your classy dressing
With your members draped in gold
Yesterday is buried
Like a deadman in his tomb
Though your tongue may reminisce
To revert back is as doom
So unite your many tongues- my friend
To a common unity
And be the person you profess you are
Not the one people think they see.

To Row Or Not To Row

Born in South Philly in 1947
The second to be born of a family of eleven
My dad worked hard he always came home tired
At times on pay day he came home late
but it never failed we always ate
Though we were poor my mom made sure
we were clean and neat when we went out doors
When I went to school I acted a fool
not knowing then that my mind was a tool
to lay a foundation for my future life
but the point I missed was to use it right
I ripped and ran with a mindless clan
which I thought was a requirement to bein' a man
we protected our turf not knowing the worth
It belonged to the city and to us became a curse
As I grew older my heart became colder
went from robbin' and stealin' to full time dealin'
and about human life I had no feelin'
I was bound to fail going from jail to jail
in criminal activity you always leave a trail
At the end of the road there's but one place to go
it's the bowels of society and called Death Row
A place of weakness and dark despair
no help for the struggling to be found there
They cry out for help in various ways
  but its tenants contribute by feeding the craze.

Compassion's spurious and love even less
debasement & indifference is the row at its
best. I wonder if there is any hope for here
I sit spirit all but broke almost at the end of
my rope condemned to die my rights revoked
Yet I maintain a subtle stand
 I might get relief through the court of man
A desperate man devises futile plans
save the body the mind demands
But the court of man cannot be bland
impartiality is their job at hand
My mind races to and fro, to live or die
I do not know but to put my trust in mortal
man I think to myself is only a sham
I could fool myself beyond a doubt
that the court of man provides an out
my brain is tired my body weak
but my mind/spirit still seek relief
Now coming to the end I see
relief had always lived in me
It was a choice I should have made
to mend my life and change my ways
There's not much more that I can tell
row a boat on a river not a jail cell to hell.

Donald Hall is on death row in Pennsylvania.

Richard Hamilton

D.O.B. 2/16/63.   Date sentenced 6/12/95.

I've been writing since I was 15 years old. I spent 15 years in the N.C. system and a year on Death Row in Fla. I'm 34 now and I feel your project is very worthwhile. I'd love to be of help to you in any way I can.

...The executioner knows no shame
America has paved his way...

Politics of Death

I've smelled the burning flesh of men
Their screams still fresh on my mind
I knew them each as my friend
together we've waited in line,
Souls that cry out in the night
such memories are mine to keep
searching the darkness I see no light
the echoes fill my sleep,
The executioner knows no shame
America has pave his way
awaiting those left in the game
the killing fields of today
I too live among the walking dead
my eyes have lost their flair
at what point will they shave my head?
when will I embrace the chair?
It's the saddest thing I've ever seen
votes that steal one's breath
during elections it's a song of extremes
It's the politics of death.

Richard Hamilton is on death row in Fla.

Demitrius Henderson

D.O.B. 11/5/67.   Date sentenced 7/2/87.

It's strickly within the power of each human being to take control of their life so the power will not land into the hands of the wrong person. I cannot change anyone but I pray that my thoughts take root inside your hearts and mind because life inside a cage is nothing to feel cool about.

   ... for every cell there is a man
   with his number.

Dust and Ruin

Castle made to bound the guilty
torn by hatred and physical strife.

Death no-longer a mystery, hunted dreams
weighted down, but lost reality.

Dappled skin dark, red, cinnamon, and pale;
original men corrupt, loyal, old, adolescence.

In my cell is the illusion of freedom each
day appears like the sunrise cascading
a foreign planet.
I awake, though my soul has fled to migrate
like the wildebeast threading
the hot African jungle for every cell,
there is a man with his number.

Eternally in flight like the clouds gathering a
storm like a voyage, my soul flew away to
the freedom I'd never see.
I almost wished that I might follow thee.
Like the broken fragments resembling the
ancient, Egyptian tomb; this castle
will crumble, and my body lay to ruin,
Dust alone can fill my belly.

Demetrius Henderson is on death row in Ill.

Barry Jones

D.O.B. 8/26/58.   Date sentenced 7/21/95.

When I was younger I thought I was sly and the law would never catch me. I would like to share a few poems with you to help you help others because if I knew 20 years ago what I know today I would not be here today.

... as I ponder these thoughts at night and begin to see my past was not right...

Innocent

There is a person dead.
This i know is true.
I cried till my eyes were red,
but know not what to do.

I had no real defense.
for a crime i had no part.
so the verdict made no sense,
but is tearing me apart.

Life means so very little
to the people on the jury.
so they put me on the middle
and condemed me in a hurry.

The judge was just a man.
with a job to carry out.
but who's to say he can.
and never have a doubt.

It is a disgrace.
I think you will agree.
to put someone in a place,
that they should never be.

Justice Is A Crime

I think of the days when i was a child
just a carefree kid, out running wild
my thoughts of the future,
were often shattered
by things in the present, that did not matter.
As i grew older, my ways were the same
I had the idea, that life was a game.
So to win i cheated, but instead i lost
and as a loser, i am paying the cost
but as i ponder, these thoughts at night
and begin to see, my past was not right
I pray for a future, that i hope will be
a way of life, that will keep me free.

Barry Jones is on death row in Arizona.

James Jones

D.O.B. 9/12/42.   Date sentenced 6/6/85.

I'd rather lived my life with no feets and no arms and hands than to lived it the way I did or as any of these guys lived. Find someone who cares about you and listen to them or I promise you'll be listening to the sounds I hear everyday.

....once a young man that could not be tamed...is now wearing a ball and chain.

This Smile Is Just For You

As the days and nights pass me by, I thank god
to be alive
As the weeks and monthes disappear, I thank
the lord through these tears that you still care
my dear.
As the years take its revenge, I know my youth
is at its end.
Once a young man that could not be tamed;
living life for glory and fame, is now wearing
a ball and chain.
My letters are few and short in length, from my
lawyer who says he needs time to think.
My friends and neighbors I can not find, since I
started doing time
My family who I loved all my life, has erased
me from their life.
As the years turn my beard from black to gray
day by day I thank the lord as I pray
that you never cast my love away.
I have lost my youth and all my tooth: almost
blind from doing time, I wonder why you
is still coming around.
Although I am smiling day by day, its not from
being in this place: Yes I must tell you the truth,
this smile is just for you.

The Lost Family

While sitting in my prison cell.
which is next door to hell
the memory of my family
is kicking down the door
as it has many times before.

Can it be true
are they thinking of me too?
fourteen years we have been apart
no wonder I'm no longer in their heart.

Wishing I could hug them
is only a dream, for their hearts
are far from me.
coming form a large family
brings back such memories...

James Jones in on death row in Pennsylvania.

Mark Lankford

D.O.B. 4/25/56. Date sentenced 10/15/84.

I have done a poem for you to utilize... most people here have lost the ability to trust and feel but I hope this helps in some way.

Until you've lived a dozen years on death row; then, my friend you will know...

Death's Stare

Do you know death
Have you seen its insipid stare?
Have you read on the written page
of the day you will die?

Have you listened to people talk
in florid terms about how it is justified
that your life be snuffed out?

Have you heard those same tortured souls
opine about how sacred life is?
About how morality is being destroyed
in our society?

About how movies and media are to blame
for all our anti-social ills?

About how the church is the answer
and can you see the cowardice of the elders
who cannot be called leaders
for they have failed to lead?
Have you heard things about yourself
from the lips of liars you know are untrue?
Have you spoken truth and no ear turned to hear
as if you and your voice were insignificant?
Have those who said they loved you abandoned
you and left you for dead?

Or lied to you when you call, to tell them
you remain alive and innocent?

Do you look into the eyes of the person
that may be your executioner
as they hand you your morning meal?

As they give you your mail and exchange
words of the weather with you?

Do you profess your innocence, If only
to reinforce your strength to carry on one
more day?

Do you know if anyone would care if you died?
Do you know that anyone cares if you live?

When you have felt these things, when you've
see and heard; when you've tasted the
bitterness of a coward's word;
when you read of the day
that you will die;
Then perhaps you can look me in the eye.
Until you've lived a dozen years
on Death Row
then my friend, you will know
you can be dead
yet live.

Mark Lankford is on death row in Idaho.

Brian Lord

D.O.B. 12/29/60.   Date sentenced 8/18/87.

I would be interested in doing whatever I could to help kids from winding up in prison. Enclosed is a poem I wrote. I want to say that what you are doing is a great thing. Please never give-up on the kids.

So what can I do to keep you far away
a little ink on paper probably won't say.

It's Not to Late for You

It seems that my twisted mind
Ticks slower and less kind.
Brain failure at its peak
This feeling each day of the week

I did drugs for the sake of fun
And now realize the damage I've done.
Livin' high and fast sure has its cost.
For the brain cells shall always be lost.
Looking at my neighbor, he's the same way
another fool on the row, what can I say.
I'm no expert, but I can say this prison life sucks
and freedom I miss.

Being under the influence you think you're in
control, The path to destruction is a simple stroll.
So when trouble stares you in the face get the heck
outta there and don't leave a trace.

Drugs lead to trouble and that ain't no good
So please pay attention or come join the hood.
And if you're cute you'll be one of those, but if
you're strong we can be bro's.
Surely you don't want that you know what I meant
All types of human derelicts especially the bent
and if you choose to ignore this advice
you'll see for yourself that it's not very nice.

For this one way ticket you won't be back,
a few more years for me and that's a fact.

Time ticks as a heart and fire burns fear,
knowing the nightmares are coming near.

So what can I do to keep you far away,
a little ink on paper probably won't say.
But if it does and I knew it would save
you from coming here,
I'd be smiling in my grave.

****

God bless those who don't enter
the abyss,
May God bless those who enter
another wish.

Brian Lord is on death row in Washington.

Jack Mazzan

D.O.B. 11/?/46. Date sentenced 1/22/78.

Ultimately, we must take full responsibility for where we are. Contributing factors can be acknowledged, but not blamed. The ultimate blame must be accepted or the process is not worth the time it took to imagine. It is a very painful and frightening process to endure alone. But the reward is great...

A motley crew they are indeed
all lined up at the bars to feed.

no title.

A stark iron room of waiting pawns
that pace 'till dawn --
around a path well worn through time
by others trapped in crime.
Time lapsed while in this darkened room-
Whilst waiting for court's doom-
Is lost, in fact, like flashing light
across the sky at night.
A piece of time sliced out of life-
neat - as by surgeon's knife-
One can't replace the time once lost-
you need not ask the cost-
just tell me of one recent day
you'd have me take away.

****

The cell; six sides; confine; surround.
The bars; stone cold; They keep me bound.
Not free; now locks will keep me here.
While night, nor day will yield life's cheer.
When thoughts; some lost, within my mind
are all I have in which to find
who live and breathes within this cell-
A man; complete; or just a shell.

Jack Mazzan is on death row in Nevada.

Angel Medrano

D.O.B. 11/28/56.   Date sentenced 8/22/88.

I am a Mexican-American, who has been doing time for the last ten years. I'm now 39 years old. My reason for writing this is quite simple. I want to help those who think it's cool to be a fool. I want them to realize that a place such as this is not what some think it to be. So don't come to prison my Brothers & Sisters, for a life here has no meaning in this world we all live in.

Prison is...

Prison is a place where you exchange the dignity of
your name for the degradation of a number...
Prison is a place where you live from visit to visit-if
you're lucky enough to have someone come visit you.

Prison is a place where you learn the countings of life:
You count the years; the seasons; months, weeks, days,
hours, minutes, and seconds as life passes you by...
Prison is a place where you hope and pray not to die...

Prison is a place where you are lucky if you never
have to kill some fool for whatever the reason...
Prison is a place where therapy and religion are not
looked upon as beneficial in a Parole Board Report...

Prison is a place where the freedom of the world can
bring tears of remembrance to the meanest of killers...
Prison is a place where the convicts wages don't
increase but the canteen prices rise to the sky...

Prison is a place where you can clearly hear the echoes
of family and friends saying "We told You So-o-o." So
don't come to prison my Brothers and Sisters, for a life
here has no meaning in this world we all live in...

Angel Medrano is on death row in Arizona.

Donald Paradis

D.O.B. 2/22/49.   Date sentenced 4/07/82.

When I received this series of poems from Mr.Paradis he was still being held on death row in Idaho and his poems are therefore included here. His sentenced was commuted to life in prison in 1996.
No additional information was provided by this inmate.

The years have come and gone so have family and friends. Most are just distant memories.

Finality

Ashes to ashes dust to dust
From dirt we came to dirt we go
But is that finality...
The innocent man lays on the table of
death, Strapped in place needle in arm
The cure of intolerance is pumped
into his veins
His eyes close... his last breath...
The doctor announces, "he has
expired" Unlike a parking meter
You cannot put in another coin
and get more time
Finality...
But is even just one remembers
and carries on
delivers his fight
He'll be like a caterpillar in his
cocoon and like a butterfly
his spirit will fly away
with great delight... Finality
Where does it come from
where does it go...
Please don't ever give into finality
continue on
Give the hope of life
Live and let live
Forevermore....

The Cell

Seen by day the cell appears like a small room
Smaller than some closets in a fine home on the hill
and smaller than the closet where the janitor keeps his
mops and brooms. As the minutes travel on their
journey to the end of the day. Night pales the friendly
glow of light. The calming sounds of day slowly
dissolve into the shadowy sounds of night.
Sleep, when it comes is a welcome friend
the echoing sounds from inside ones head
Make the ones outside seem like chimes
from a carousel. Oh the eerie sounds of despair...
No one can hear you scream inside your own head.
A rose bush of thoughts and rusted memories
cling to the inside of your skull like barnacles
to the hull of a long docked ship at some
out of the way, forgotten wharf. You know that
the time in this isolation will change you
and that you can't change time....
Sitting in the dark wondering about the unknown
chains you to a wall of doubts and fear
No one likes to admit their fears
through the day you put on the air of strength
the night brings sorrow and weakness to all
Yes even the unbeliever prays and begs God at night
to deliver them from the phantoms of their mind.
In the deep dark inner recesses of the prison cell even
tough guys cry in the dark... I turned to see a little bird
looking at me through my cell window... I am
haunted by the tears in its eyes as it looked at me.

Mail

Mail call I heard the guard yell-out on the tier
in a cold raspy tone of agitation and indif-
ference I didn't even stir.
I've heard that same call five days a week
for fourteen and a half years now.
Years ago that sound would bring me to new
life each day.
The letters and cards were many and full of
life and hope...
From family and friends some just well-
wishers. The years have come and gone
so have family and friends.
Most are just distant memories...
But this day was different
The footsteps stopped in front of my cell door
I could see his shadow interrupt the light
that squeezed through the crack under the
door I heard it before I saw it slide across the
floor I just sat there and stared at it
Unbelievably, for what seemed forever...
I must have fallen asleep.
When I woke up I thought it was a dream,
looking at the floor I realized that it wasn't,
The envelope was there....

Empty

If you close your eyes what do you see
The tops of snow capped mountains
A butterfly fluttering on the breeze
A lone tree standing
on wind swept plain
Children dancing freely in a meadow
Blanketed with flowers of many colors...
When I close my eyes all I see is concrete and steel
Men in transparent boxes
Tormented by self pity and pain
Bludgeoned by nightmares and thoughts
Wishing that they, with their eyes opened
Could see all that you do with closed eyes
With eyes opened they walked through this life
Not seeing, not feeling, not knowing...
I saw a man sitting in his cell one day with a piece of
drawing paper and paints and brushes in front of
him I asked what he was going to paint, with a blank
stare he said, "A picture."
A few days later I went by his cell again and noticed
he was still sitting there
with the blank paper in front of him.
I asked him why he hadn't started yet.
He looked at me with a tear in his eye and said,
"I don't remember what things look like...."

My Friend

Words in my callused heart do not flow freely
From my lips... Here I have only one true friend
My pen
Opening its mouth it speaks
The hidden treasures of my soul
Can you feel my silent voice
Speaking from the paper
Like pollen floating in the womb of the night
My pen opens its mouth
Speaking in tones of slow whispers and hulking laughter.
Sometime screaming with pain
Tears from its eye cover the paper
Like a soaring eagle often times unnoticed
My pen transmits me from a world of dreams
To a world of stark reality... and back again
Reality that is shrouded with Cellophane hopes and barbed wire dreams
Flowing... the blood from its heart
My pen extends its warm, loving hands
It guides my way like a compassionate mother
Through sunshine and rain. Sometimes when I can't sleep, my pen calms me with the lullaby that it sings
I can taste its milk
Filled with its motherly love
My pen is my company where others have fled...

On the Inside

Do you live your life on the outside...
Always putting your best plastic foot forward
Keeping the real you in chains
Being your own jailer...
When one hears the words, "on the inside"
The first thought that comes to mind is
Prison; towering walls, guntowers, steel-bars,
barbedwire And gun toting guards
Very few think of the unseen being
The soul, the house of true motivation...
Have you ever smiled & said something nice to
someone, But on the inside knew differently
Or made a compromise that on the inside knew
Was wrong for you...
Like after kissing ass washing out your mouth
Because of the bad taste it leaves
And you think to yourself.. that person isn't who I am
That's living on the outside
The real prison and chains...
Inside is where the freedom is
Brake the door down
The plastic will melt
The chains will brake
Your jailer will flee
You will gain confidence in yourself
And people will regain respect for you
Right or wrong you will be able to
Live comfortably with yourself...

Donald Paradis is in prison in Idaho.

David Pellegrini

D.O.B. ?/?/66.　Date sentenced 7/23/87.

If hell was a worldly place it'd be prison. The inmates occasionally stab each other & guards with whatever they can make to do so. Inmates get raped,beat and killed by inmates either individually or by groups.So if you like living in a controlled environment with a bunch of rats you'll love it here.If you hate freedom and don't give a damn about any one but yourself this is the place to be.

Prison is A Pit

Prison is a pit
A hole of dark disgust
You always watch your back
For no one can you trust.

The days go on forever
Time records you've lost
Ruthlessness abounds
In seeking to accost.

Never can you rest in peace
For peace they'll give you not
Better, yea to keep your life
Then freedom have ye not.

Vile darkness swoons about
Depression fills the air
Death can come not soon enough
To end the long despair.

D. Pellegrini is on death row in Nevada.

Delores Rivers

D.O.B. 12/25/53. Date sentenced 3/16/89.

What is it like being on Death Row? It's hard lock-up time, being treated like an animal in a cage with people looking at you all the time. It's really crazy here. I want to share my story with these kids.

People are yelling and fighting each other searching and losing and becoming more smothered.

A Facade of Happiness

Here in this prison my heart is torn;
trampled to pieces by the public's scorn.
There's hardly a moment when I'm happy
inside. When I'm scared or confused
in my cell will I hide. But these walls are no
comfort for the pain I bare or the heartache
or loneliness or the despair.
Where is the peace and contentment I seek?
My body and soul are ever so weak.
Nobody can know what I feel inside;
the torment and anguish in a teenagers cry.
The nights bring quietness but never the peace;
that my broken soul fervently seeks.
The tears that stain my pillow - they burn;
yet are never ending they always return.
My mind tells me one thing - my heart another.
This facade of happiness is my hideous cover.
People are yelling and fighting each other;
searching and losing and becoming more
smothered. They want to die and escape the
pain to give up completely yet die in shame.
I need a good friend on whom I can depend
Someone to pick me up a helping hand to
lend. Where are the answers
but what are the questions
Won't someone please save me
from this lonely depression ?

A Lonely Look Out The Window

As I sit in my chair in a lonely room.
I feel something sweeping over me,
hurt and pain captures me.
The depths of sadness have flooded my
soul. I have this strong desire to search
the clouds for that comfort that I lost
in the shadows.
The wind knocks on my window.
I stand with my eyes closed and
the cool winter breeze brushes over
my face and through my hair.
As I open my eyes, I see these beautiful
stars shining about the room.
They seem like real people smiling at me,
saying we love you!
Tears start rolling down my cheeks.
I feel the stars catching and wiping away
my silent tear drops that no one sees of
this lonely person sitting in the room
with nothing
but the clouds
and the stars
and God's nature as her friend.

Touching Life

A Bird races across the sky,
he hears the wind he feels the
slightest movement of the trees.

Longing for understanding...
He soars to the sky, the warmth
of the clouds floods his wings
for a moment they cloud his vision,
but yet the warmth of his inner self,
feels their lightness.
floating into a new direction,
he never fears, but only enjoys all
that it's giving for that moment.
Slowly the warmth of the clouds
moves away lightly and coldly
he begins to look further longing
for that feeling he once felt
another cloud comes by, this time
he doesn't have to ask, Why ?

Delores Rivers is on death row in Penn.

Steven Roach

D.O.B. 4/10/76.   Date sentenced 5/10/95.

Sometimes I'm very discouraged, the road seems long and narrow. I am currently on deathrow in VA. I was 17 years old when charged with capital murder and given a death sentence after my 18th birthday. I have enclosed 4 poems that I wrote while on deathrow.

Remember Me

Prison's no place for an innocent child.
There's no room for the meek, nor mild.

The nights are so lonely I toss in my bed
The days are so weary I face them with dread.

Grant me one prayer as you did on the cross
for that thief who knew his life was a loss.

Please come to this prison where I sit alone
surrounded by razor wire, guards and stone.

Broken and penitent, forgotten and lost
on the ash heap of regret
where my life is tossed.
I've no other place left on this earth
remember me o Lord renew my birth.

Come to this prison enter my cell
save me, forgive me, in this
man-made Hell

And if in this life, no home here I see
In your Kingdom of forgiveness Lord
remember me!

In Jail With the Lord

Alone one night
In shame and despair.
I looked for help
But none was there.

No future... but prison
No past....... but pain.

I look in the mirror
my tears the rain.

By justice condemned
in time to die.
my only hope, God's mercy
for his grace did I cry.
Then a seed planted
somewhere long ago.

In the midst of my pain
I began to grow.

Faith

Faith is holding on to life.
When all around is pain.
Faith is seeing rainbows,
When the sky is full of rain.

Faith is reaching out for God,
When you're filled with fear.
Faith is taking someone's hand,
And feeling the Lord is near.

Faith is walking in the dark,
And looking for the light.

Faith is knowing God is love,
And that you truly care.
Faith is searching for the Lord,
And finding Him in your heart.

Steven Roach is on death row in Virginia.

Fred Robinson

D.O.B. 5/3/41.   Date sentenced 11/18/88.

If this is what you want to hear I will help you because I got kids myself and I send them poems to remember me by, so if this will help some kid get his life together it will make me happy.

who will bury me,
burn the meat from my bones,
crying tears for my last dying moans?

What is My Name

If I should die tonight who would remember me?
Who will bury me, burn the meat from my bones.
Crying tears from my last dying moans?
Is anyone out there?
Does anyone hear the creaking of my heart
as loneliness steals my soul bit by bit?
Still breathing, why can't I quit?
Raging inhabitant of societies disease
my bones running liquid,
my heart grown hard,
senses throbbing darkly with infection.
Voices whispering in my head
with no inflection.
That cool valley of peace found to be a mirage lost
completely in illusions misty shores.
Who will cry for my passing?
In the distance I hear steel doors crashing
then I do not hear. Nothing.

Fred Robinson Sr. is on death row in Arizona.

Richard Shere

D.O.B. 7/7/66. Date sentenced 4/17/89.

I am not a poet and I don't like to read poetry, but I am an artist and I usually do well at everything, & God inspired me to write to help the kids. I hope I've been helpful.

Am I not worthy, have they no compassion, is my life worth so little, can they not see my tears..?

A Night in Prison

My head hits the pillow, as I try to fall asleep
I hear the screams from this place
to keep me awake
Fear rushes upon me more and more
that I may be next and I begin to cry
only to awake to a cold disgusting meal
my heart in my throat
so angry I won't talk to no one for hours
only to keep my mouth shut and obey my
masters commands the rest of the Day.
The cold hateful guards and prisoners
who do not care and would only like to
rape you hurt you and kill you with pipes,
knives and aids.
Even eye contact is a threat
so I dare not look for comfort
because it is not to be found
not in prison
not in the tears on my pillow.

Richard Shere is on death row in Florida.

Willie Sullivan

D.O.B. ?/?/75.   Date sentenced 12/30/93.

No additional information was provided by this inmate.

Tell me why everyone
 wants to go to heaven
 but no one wants to die.

A Letter To God

Look into my eyes and see the tears I cry.
Touch my body and feel the misery inside.
Dear Father tell me why, why have I seen
so many come and seen so many go.
and had to pray for people I don't know.
I wonder why evil keeps knocking at my door
Should I answer it, sometimes I just don't know

It seems that I am losing this fight
for all the things I thought was right
I once thought I had seen the light
only to be pulled back into the night
I'm calling on you Jesus Christ,
to please help me to understand what is right.
Please pull me back into the light.
Why does one man take another ones life?
If by God that ain't right
I pray for ill, those who live in this life
for all those who do and don't believe
in Jesus Christ.

Tell me why everyone wants to go to heaven
but no one wants to die.
Why can't our dreams become reality
How come reality seems more like a nightmare
Tell me why the grass is green
Tell me why humans feel pain
and in the spring it rains.

Why can't fish live on land.
Tell me why God created man
Why, I just don't understand.

As I kept looking beyond the clouds
I saw my father's face,
As he looked down at me and said,
"Son, don't lose the faith."
He then disappeared from sight.
His voice was tender and light
it was the words of Jesus Christ.

Please Father hear my prayers
to bless everyone and forgive
our sins as we're only humans
Who Don't Understand.

Willie Sullivan is on death row in Delaware.

John Szabo

D.O.B. 2/13/58.   Date sentenced 10/3/79.

I am quite interested in assisting the turning around of today's youth so they do not have to suffer the same pitfalls which I suffered. Also, know that I do not write any poetry which even comes close to being preachy.

   These bars are for caged animals-
   Our keepers hold the keys;

Todays Never End

Tumultuous souls in multitudes-
Abandoned... the common denominator-
As years go by even more souls die;
The process is ineluctable.
They come, they go-
They live, they die-
All ineffably altered;
There's a turnstile to admit us all-
Existence horrifically changed.

Time runs out on all of us-
The pariahs as we are called!
Our parents die without our presence-
Permission to attend a funeral;
Not granted by the boss.
We're treated like disposable chattel-
Double handcuffed, chained and shackled-
Told when to eat, sleep, shit and shower-
Humiliated at the people's disgust
toward us.
We exist within a living death-
I await for that sweet release!
If there truly is a hell, be told'
It's behind these bars and walls of cold.
The sun does not shine with life's intensity-
All life has been drained far away;

The walking surely are dead... Within!
Prison is the biggest functional morgue-
Flowers cease to exist for us-
Love... but a distant memory-
Squirrels don't run in the parks these days;
Our parks are fenced cages of barbed wire!
When it snows, it doesn't-
When it rains, it's dry-
When it's hot we all rot in hell!
When stars come out we just can't say-
For all our days are darkened hells.

All our dreams turned nightmares-
Desires are left behind;
We live in the moment
without tomorrows
Todays Never End!
Picture a world of barked orders-
Your worst nightmare cannot compare!
Picture a world of endless tomorrow's;
Your Todays Never End-
Todays Never End!
It's only the beginning...
Todays Never End!

Time In The Bricks

Behind these walls of solitude-
Hell within each brick!
The failure's pain and abandonment-
A world of discontent.
These bars are for caged animals-
Our keepers hold the keys;
The Judge deals out our ultimate fate...
Death!
Hard Time In The Bricks.

Time goes by as standing still-
We're like cattle on two feet!
Minds are stagnant-
Souls are lost-
Part of progress we surely are not.
Society says to "Lose the keys-
We're tired and we're scared;
Lock them up or take their lives,
As they have taken so many souls."
Time In The Bricks...
You can lose yourself!
To survive we all must change;
Seventy-nine to present day-
This world is so damn strange.
I'm a autodidact by need to grow-
The desire to become whole;

My mind's a sponge for knowledge lost-
So I read and study from morn to morn;
Time In The Bricks has surely scarred
my soul.
I busy myself to block out the horrors:
The rapes!
The deaths!
The wars!
I better myself to be accepted...
By America's societal bores.
The keepers of the keepers of the keepers
of the keys -
The keepers who watch us shit!
I'll only content myself when my freedom's
gained.
Or my life is drained away!
But I'll not allow my mind to die.
Nor be a recidivist to Time In The Bricks.

Behind these walls is hell on earth-
I'm in the Devil's cage!
Man condemning man each day-
Continued through the nights.
Time In The Bricks;
A lifeless life!
A world of only dark-
A sure way in with so few out-
Time In The Bricks I can do without.

Judgment Day

I'm on my way to the death-house
My spirit to be taken away
It's nothing new to me, though,
Because you took my soul the other day.
I've been judicially dead since '79'
Surviving day to day
My heart was turned to granite stone
My spirit and soul are now but ghosts.
I'm nothing but a walking shell
Hollow as a memory!
I'm not too sure just where I'm going
Will it be Heaven or the depths of hell?
The sun is disappearing
My fire is all but out
What's left is a glimmer of what once was
Still slowly slipping way and away.

I thought my fire would be rekindled
When she came in to my life
But what she left I carry forever
In my heart she buried another cold knife.
Death will be a sweet release
No more bullshit games!
I'll leave with a smile saying good-bye-

Kiss my ass you tripe.
I'll leave in the manner in which I came
Quiet and all alone
A living enigma cherished by none
Yet even the deaf can hear my heart's moans.

The day is drawing near!
The gates are opening wide
And still the one whom holds my heart
Is nowhere close but lost inside.

No more bullshit games!
I'll go out with a smile
Saying "Fuck you" to the world of fools
All the crooked people and their lies.

The sun has finally set now
It's just moments from the slay
"Good-bye, my love," I say to you
On this, my final Judgment Day.

John Szabo is on death row in Illinois.

D. B. Teague

D.O.B. 11/11/62. Date sentenced 11/11/86.

I hope that my poems will help a kid in some way. Maybe they will learn to use all of that pent up energy and anger in a more creative way. You shouldn't have to go to prison just to learn you have talent.

...I'll meet the Great Spirit and say my farewells, But I'll never forget that long narrow trail...

Freedom

Freedom is breathing
all the air you can.
Freedom is walking
for miles in the sand.
But how can this be
when I am locked within
No longer among my friends
will this nightmare ever end.
Freedom is understanding
all that is around.
Freedom is conversing
without making a sound.
freedom is being able
to speak your own mind.
Freedom is always searching
for someone you might find.
But how can this be
when freedom is just a word.
A word in prison
that is not even heard.

I Search

The days are much warmer
The nights are much colder
The ages of time,
Just keep getting older.
The seasons come, as the years go.
The raindrops are of sorrow
As my loneliness begins to show.
As I continue my search
throughout the human race.
I search for happiness
and peace of mind
I search for a love
that I once left behind
I search for the secrets of immortality
A way out of this fantasy in reality.

The Cycle

I wake up and here I am
Time to work once more.
I look around and nothing has changed;
Those menacing walls are still here,
Standing tall and strong.
Adjusting to this routine isn't easy.
As my mind drifts away.
My thoughts have traveled;
Surely my friend, you must know where.
The day was long but aren't they all?
My work is done for now.
Time to relax although I don't see how.
But wait, night has fallen, what a relief
Because before another day arrives
I shall go home tonight.
For they can hold my person,
But never my dreams.
I wake up and...

Another Mountain

There's going to be another mountain
A mountain to climb and to find.
Five years; A lifetime
Two hundred miles far.
She stands tall, unconquered.
She's in my thoughts in my dreams
And in my future.
Together we will rise
Striving for the summit
Of yet what lies untold.
Experience is never an omen
It speaks only truth.
It must be endured
To its very peaks.
There are mountains enough
For all to climb.
But for the few who find
Forever the memory of
Their experience lives.
To find oneself
Is to find yet another mountain
A mountain to climb.

Long Narrow Trail

Branded on my mind
A memory there to stay
A vision of small clearing
And a long narrow trail.
It's a quarter mile to the clearing
Down this long narrow trail of gray.
A quarter mile back
I prepare to meet the trail
For many years I'll walk
this long narrow trail
With the blowing of the breeze
And the birds in the trees.
You can walk forever
down this long narrow trail
And when you reach the end
You have gone nowhere at all.
I get up every morning
and wait for the dawn
Then I start the journey
down the long narrow trail.
But one glad morning
as the years begin to fail
I'll take my last journey down
That long narrow trail.
I'll meet the Great Spirit and say my farewells
But I'll never forget that long narrow trail.

What The Clouds See

A warrior crouches
in the forest
waving a tree
branch.
He screams, "Bang"
and a transparent
soldier falls
to the ground.

We can't see
the soldiers; but
the warrior swears
they are there.
In fact, his horse
the wind, has
just smelled
another...
Therefore, since the branch
is pointing right at us,
we marvel at the solider's
death and quickly
float away.

Brothers of The Clan

I sit by the river and listen
To the rustle of the wind.
I hear dead warriors voices
Calling my name again.
I look up into the blue
With tears in my eyes.
Hoping to see heaven's horsemen
ride across the skies.
I think of Red Fox, Gray Wolf
and Hawk, Warriors tried and true.
Their embraces of the Owl Clan
And the good times that we knew.
We rode together, Brothers of the Clan
Someday, Brothers
We'll ride together again.

D.B Teague is on death row in Texas.

Norman Timberlake

D.O.B. 8/?/47.   Date sentenced 8/11/95.

I agree that kids today need blunt truth to sincerely know where their headed and it does take seeing from the end of where they could end if they don't wish to change for themselves. T.V. glamorizes crime and there is no glamour upon death row.

God is silent, no letters do I receive no one calls or visits me. Nothing else do I have but one envelope to thee.

untitled

I guess it all comes down to what is right
not so much what I've done but what I
should've done.
And I guess it all comes down that you
are right not to condemn me for what I
haven't done, but for what I should've done
But when you've always been alone
and nothing else has anyone truly shown,
you drink to despair to forget.
And live in moments as they truly should be
but when you see the light isn't there
the alcohol helps out the despair to forget
So what do I do now my child when truly
I am very alone and death haunts my every
day when I have not the drink to forget
nor a voice to hear when death seems
the only way God is silent, no letters do I
receive no one accepts calls or visits me
nothing else do I have
but one envelope to thee
Poems of a sad life to one I love more
then she knows
hopefully this will say
I do understand how,
now do you see.

untitled #2

Today a man was given a piece of paper
the most important in his life
That set a date thirty days off
that the state would take his life.

And I heard him say
this means nothing to me
You've already destroyed me
At least now from all this I'll finally be free

So I sat on my bunk & sincerely tried to understand, what just came in what could bring this
to this man, To no longer wish to fight or to live
And then it dawned;
nowhere else to appeal was his
For fifteen years he had tried to explain
and without no real help, it is a shame
To sit back and watch him for the last days
Lost beyond all hope, nothing further to say.

I'm here for a much more publicized crime
And for something I have not done but a guard
tells me he hears this all the time
And as I think upon how much more
seriously they wish to kill me
I wonder for how long until me.

untitled#3

Who will ever know
who will ever understand
who will ever care
who will ever be there
to love me instead of stare.

Who was it that caused this
who was it that blamed me
who was it they let walk out the door
who was it they forgot
As I sit back enduring days until they kill me.

Who was the Judge over looking the law
who was the Prosecutor that used lies
who was it that didn't defend me
who was it that convicted me
As now all block appeals to rightfully free me.

Who will ever know
who will ever understand
who will ever care
who will ever there be
to love me, instead of stare?

Norman Timberlake is on death row in Ind.

Johnny Townsend

D.O.B. 12/63.   Date sentenced 3/8/85.

I read your letter asking for assistance in opening our children's eyes. Because I've missed out on my own child's life, I feel that it is my duty to at least try to save someone elses. With that in mind, [here's] three of my poems for a most important cause.

Mentally, physically, spiritually
tattered, suffering from mankind's
evil and overbearing nature:

In Bondage

Isolated into a galaxy of my imagination,
a place exploding
with the illusion of being free.

Suffering, because afraid to take a chance
to journey into the light.

What awaits me there? A voice answers,
" Go and feast your eyes, only then shall you
understand the reason for being in bondage."
Traveling down a long corridor,
coming closer and closer to a door marked,
'Clearing Mist', I hesitated before opening it;
the passion for insight was delayed once
more as another question was asked,
Are you sure you want the truth?
Yes, I answered. I burst through the door
& there They stood along side of confession.

Captured by the depths of my soul, complete
with a mirror image broken by a force;
Truth.
I fell into a shattered and miserable life.

Innocent Cries From The Shadows

Weary cries rise out of the dark and lonely shadows of
night, like a cold and chilling wind...
Children, standing alone, to the side, out of the way lost
and forgotten, with empty bellies and clouded minds,
eyes dark and hollow, filled with tears...
Soulful arms outstretched, wanting, needing, desiring
to be touched by human kindness, to be filled with
purpose, with love, with total understanding; all un-
conditionally mentally, physically, spiritually tattered,
suffering from mankind's evil and overbearing nature:
Infected, a destructively horrendous disease, a sickness
of all take and absolutely no give, of innocence lost,
gone forever...Man's ability to destroy life, many a
child's life, without even a thought, without any
feeling, by deeds, by cold-hearted, hateful ways
that are beyond all understandings of a child...
Destruction at the hands of greedy, mindless,
uncaring souls that leave a trail of death wherever
they may tread, souls that have left a world cold,
barren and desolate. An isolated place where great and
mighty castles once stood proud, strong, and majestic...
Once so bright, so busy, like a cool well that springs up
from the desert, now gone dry and dead from age and
neglect... Cities lay in heaps, useless rubble like so
many faded and forgotten dreams and lives through-
out the ages... The destructive hands of wicked souls
reach out into each and every direction; West, North,
East and South, deadly hands with a poisonous touch...

Many new kingdoms to conquer, lands to
dispose of, dreams to be crushed, the backs
of children to walk upon, lives to be lost,
controlled abused and disrupted, to be thrown
into the trash heap, more innocence lost...
As I an adult soul, stand within my own
clouded mind, looking out through my eyes,
the portholes of my being a wasted existence
appear before me where great potential once
lived, death, where life once flourished, pain
& suffering, past & present, future an eternity
in our path... A frightening thought, this
troubled land, created from the depths of
man's ignorance, the very madness that is his
life. The sight of children laying by the wayside
never having left their mark on history, never
having made any great contributions to society
as a whole... A future gone! Death now fills the
spaces that were once occupied by life, love has
become hate, lies replace truth, and peace has
died, allowing war to prevail, and as always the
children suffer... Death a relentless creature of
habit, created by the designs of mankind's
wickedness, walks the face of the world and
has for many millennia, devouring life at will
in its steely powerful jaws. Like a phantom it
wreaks havoc & lays waste to precious creation
it crumbles castled cities, destroying all that
is good, pure and perfect, and now as before,
history continues at a frantic and hellish pace.

Innocent Cries From The Shadows
(continued)

Deaths certain will cannot and shall not last forever...
Changes can and need be made if life is to move
forward with any hope of being better...

Better; if not for everyone, at least for the children,
our children...
Could it? Shall it ever happen? Will we ever see it
come to pass?
The answer is a resounding NO! Not unless we begin
treating all children with the utmost love and respect
that they so deserve...
Not unless we reach out with love, understanding and
human kindness to the children and touch their hearts
and let their innocence touch ours...
Not unless we honor, protect and save their innocence
Not unless we all stop and listen and truly hear the
precious children cry out from the dark and lonely
shadows...

Dedicated to all the children of the world, past, present and
future... May the children of the past sleep in peace, may the
children of the present be treated with dignity and respect,
and may the children of the future never know the pain
of those who have walked before them.

The Tomb

I always thought a slow death would be painful
But this isolated slow death is of a greater agony.
In this tomb of mine, the blood drips from the
walls and the air forms, smiles and runs away.

In here there are so many voices
so many voices I hear.
I reach out in speech like so many others
But deaf ears hear not the cry for help.
And as I look around my tomb
I see so much hatred that has now formed
a place where innocence once dwelled.

And if all of this was not enough
I can hear the sound of another tomb
being placed on top of mine-
to let me know that freedom will once again...
pass me by.

Johnny Townsend is on death row in Indiana.

Mario Trevino

D.O.B. 7/25/62.   Date sentenced 7/10/84.

I've always kinda wanted to help kids that thought it was cool to do all that crazy stuff and have no clue that they're sealing their fate to a life worse than death.

My time has come to its end and I'll soon be gone: I hope with all my heart my words will carry on.

Tears of Sorrow

Clouds pass by my window
colorful birds go flying by.
Somewhere within my memory
I often ask myself why.
My life was precious
and I threw it all away,
My tears of sorrow
cloud my eyes
every single day.

Hell

The drive up is filled with anxiety
thoughts of horror and fear;
Nothing can prepare you
for when you finally arrive here.
Razor wire upon the fence
Brick, concrete and steel:
Welcome to your new home
Yeah, Hell is for real!

Hear My Words

I've seen me come and go
Death doesn't discriminate:
If you arrive to the row
You've already sealed your fate.

There are no tough guys here
we await with anticipation;
All in the same boat
This is the reality of this situation.

On borrowed time we sit
with every turn of the hourglass:
The day will soon come
When my Death will come to pass.
 I dread it with constant fear
Tears often cloud my eyes;
Nowhere to run, nowhere to go
Why did I listen to all those lies?

My time has come to its end
and I'll soon be gone:
I hope with all my heart
My words will carry on.

Mario Trevino is on death row in Texas.

Robert Turner

D.O.B. 4/12/59. Date sentenced 7/2/86.

I don't really know if I could write anything to change the minds of kids, I just don't know. What can one say to change that, but I know it's a rough life in here and it's no place for anyone.

And I never thought, it would happen to me. Being locked away for years.

I Never Thought

Well I never thought
that I would get caught
I had no troubles
no worries, no fears.

And I never thought
it would happen to me.

Being locked away for years.

12 years have gone by
as I look in the mirror
at the gray
and the lines on my face.
And all of my childhood
has withered and died
from the horrors
I've seen in this place.

The beatings
The stabbings
The everyday rape
it's hard
just trying to get by.

I've seen men
that were killed in their cells
and some were in front of the guards.

And you're coming here
You'd better be bad
Because I'm telling you
life here is hard.

No one will help you
and you're on your own
and you better be
as bad as you think.

Because when you walk thru that gate
You step into Hell
and the demons here
will just take.

And They will take you off the face of the earth.

Robert Turner in on death row in Illinois.

Herb Underwood

D.O.B. 7/?/60.   Date sentenced 8/23/85.

I may have another chance if I get it, I will not do anything wrong ever again not even jaywalking, these twelve years of hell, rapes stabbings, murders and being treated like a dog, being told when to sleep, shit and eat is real fun. You kids keep on and you can have this wonderful life also.

My future plans that I thought so well are in a dream I would like to sell.

Prison

I welcome sleep
For it brings a new Day
the past mistakes
For which I pay

My future plans
that I thought so well
are all in a dream
I would like to sell

My freedom shut
As I think each Day
of those who took
so much away
And I pray to God
that when I'm out
there will never be
without a Doubt
Another Judgment Day.

H. Underwood is in prison in Indiana. His sentence was commuted in 1997 but this poem was written while he was still on death row and is therefore included in this collection.

Robert West

D.O.B. 12/12/61.   Date sentenced 2/3/83.

I was on PCP and drinking, full of hate from two previous trips to prison and numerous stays in detention centers and reform school. All that added up to a night of madness that I have no way of changing. It doesn't mean that I'm not sorry now, I am.. I understand...

>A child will only learn,
>what it has been taught.
>So use your time and patience
>or a monster you will wrought.

Johnny Got A Gun

When I'm dead and gone, I don't want you to cry
I don't want those tears to fill your loving eyes.
Tears should not be shed for the one that passed
away, The price for life is death its a price we all
must pay. The tears should go to those who have
been left behind. Because they're the only ones
who suffer in the mind. The mind should not
suffer we celebrate its birth.
Life comes from death, destiny decides its worth.
Though the body loses form the soul forever
flies. While flying it is searching for a little better
high. When we leave this world we come back
as a child. So please don't hurt the children before
you think awhile. The child you are hurting might
remember his last life. And fill your wretched days
with unbearable forms of strife. Lets listen to the
moral then try to live it out. Before you hit the
children choose a different route. A child will only
learn what it has been taught. So use your time
and patience or a monster you will wrought.
Johnny was born in 61, a creation of sexual lust,
His parent's were both victims, back when they
were young, At times they would beat him till
his tiny ears rung. When Johnny turned 19 he
was alone and on the run.
For a fifty dollar bill he bought himself a gun.

Since he hustled dope and played the game so fast. Everyone that knew him knew he wouldn't last. By 1981 he'd been in prison twice. The things that he was taught there wasn't very nice. Rehabilitation is a word and nothing more. When one comes out of prison he's meaner then before. Johnny moved in with a hooker he had met. But even though he fell in love his hurt he could not forget. One wild Friday night he robbed a liquor store. He shot down the clerk for $40 dollars and a quart. The next day in the paper he read what he had done. He thought about his lover then looked into the sun. As time went by his hustle grew along with the odds against him. The memories of the smiles he had were quickly growing dim. His down-fall came all too fast along with summer's end.
He found the ones he thought he loved were only fair-weather friends. His girl got stabbed and beat while screwing for some bucks. It was then that Johnny seen he was running out of luck. Johnny tracked the man that had taken his ladies life. Ignoring all his pain ignoring all his strife. He found him in a bar room where the lights were turned down low. Who Johnny was the stranger didn't know. Johnny stuck his gun in a paper sack. Then made him leave the bar room with the revolver in his back. He took him to a dead-end of an alley down the street. He beat him in the head and stomped him with his feet. When Johnny finally shot him the police had just arrived they gave him the option to go dead or go alive. In a moment he decided to take it to the wire. Smiling at the pigs, he pointed then he fired...

A Ticket To Hell

The day was as hot as a witches box
and the waves on the sea stood still.
I stuck around when the gray waters
parted and the demons rose up for the
kill. Echoes rose from way down below
as Satan took command once again.
Leaches and maggots sprayed from his
mouth while he rubbed human shit on
his skin.
From the depths they came lacking a name
and their souls followed close behind.
The thunder cracked as maggots attacked
the answers no one could find
My heart skipped a beat at the sound of the
beast as he screamed for the end of time.
Then from out of the sun came the only
one that could match Satan's bloody
design.
From the blue skies cover came Satan's
mother waving a staff full of thorns.
From her body hung chunks of dung
from which Satan was literally torn.
A mad-man growled as Satan howled
spewing leaches from his asshole and
head.
As quick as a flash he jumped on her ass
hissing the lore of the dead.

My mind wasn't set to lay down a bet
but this is a fucking sure winner.
Satan looked good as I figured he would
as he ate his Mother for dinner.

The demons in flight cheered in delight
when Satan bit off half her tit.
Her blood from within now
dripped down his chin
thats when I had to split.

When finally I reached the top of the crest
I heard the doomed souls screaming detest.
Satan then turned and looked up my way

In a curse from hell I heard him say
"Maybe you think you've escaped me now
in the future you will see.
As long as you live a wicked life
your path will lead you to me.
Taking this and taking that,
is not what life's all about.
You could have everything or nothing
at all, but still you would snivel and pout.
Material addicts listen close, stay away
from the wishing-well.
Because while you're looking for shit you
don't need, I'll be pulling you closer to hell.

The Dream Makers Wall

You are the dream I dream at night
I hold your body near.
I run my fingers through your hair
while I whisper in your ear.

My heart is like the spiders web
weaved inside my soul.
You're the meal its trapped for me
how I pray its silk will hold.

The beauty of this world is ours
when we embrace each other tight.
We live inside a wonderland
protected by the night.

I feel your warmth encircle me
while we sing our names out loud
Together we celebrate our love
in the dreamers misty cloud.
As long as we keep these dreams
and never let them die
we'll always be together
like the earth wrapped in the sky.

We'll meet in our secluded world
away from reality.
In that place we call a dream

we'll hide from the eyes that see.
In that place we'll always be
together in mind and soul.
And it'll ease our minds
as we walk with time
down life's elusive roads.

Back in our thoughts,
beyond the screams
we find ourselves,
living our dreams
Holding each other,
without being there
we meet in this world,
that only we share.
And in this world, together we find
we have no heartaches,
in this world in our mind.

Sometimes, I think those dreams
are really not dreams at all.
They're glimpses of a love that thrives
from behind The Dream Makers Wall...

Robert West is on death row in Texas.

Robert Williams

D.O.B. ?/?/37.   Date sentenced 6/30/78.

No additional information was provided by this inmate.

Complacently relinquishing their culture and manhood while their women and children cringe.
How long will Brothers indirectly in complicity, assist ignorance and remain indifferently neutral on the fringe?

Prisoners of Color

You see stories written on hollow faces like
strokes. Telling a pathetic history of many
dashed hopes. Of a people too long battered,
pummeled against the ropes, those sad blank
stares of people bearing heavy yokes.
Their gods are sex, money and the sport popes
Which to a man would unanimously get their
votes.
Heritage, culture and the struggle to them
a hoax. They'd trade all for the approval
from the ruling folks.
Many seek relief through fantasies, day dreams
and soaps
or avoiding the inevitable collision with reality
with jokes.
While others pursue unrequited love
the kind that chokes
some spin elaborate yarns of their many past
cloaks...
But there's a remnant that stands above the
dopes, who utilize this time to ascend
societies' rocky slopes.
Remembering their past,
yet not bound by slave boats
Upon release, they'll become
one of the community spokes.

Utu

I've heard those eerie, lonesome, haunting wails
gurgling up from the murky ocean floors.
Poignant, mournful groans
strewn from America to the African shores.

I've seen apparitions of grotesque corps
tarred and feathered by ignorance
suspended from trees.
They petition God to hear their supplications
and as in Abel's time
He does not fail to hear their pleas.

Today the pale progeny of ignorance still reigns
...on different steeds
But the same old equestrians
seeking to perpetuate their ignorance
How long will brothers be
divided, passive pedestrians?

Complacently relinquishing their culture and manhood
While their women and children cringe?
How long will brothers indirectly in complicity
assist ignorance...
and remain indifferently, neutral...
on the fringe?

Robert Williams is on death row in Nebraska.

The Mindfield

What drove you to snatch
the breath
from their bodies?
Who pushed you to drive that spike
in your arm?
What critical part of your life
was so shattered
you unscrewed the lightbulb
and walked into the dark?

Was it tv, your daddy,
an aunt or a sitter
who kept changing stations
love, secrets, guilt, rage?

And what about you
do you remember the first time
you were trolling for answers
and hit the big snag?
Did you tug and pull gently
and try to retrieve it
or just clench your fist
till the tension went slack?

Did you know you could heal
if you took off the bandage
or did festering memories

keep gnawing you back?
Then comes the point when
you know you're mistaken
you didn't crossover-
you erased the line.
Did you increase the dosage
to numb your own feelings
or like Allen in *Equus*
did you gouge out their eyes?

Did you wait until night
like your cousin Hyena
or work as the media says
in broad light?

And now that you're caught
will you grab on to Jesus and
keep dragging him down
as you struggle and fight?
Or will you introduce
all your victims and demons
and relax as your savior
pulls all the straps tight?

Timothy Moxley is the editor
and author of this poem.

Epilogue

In compiling this collection of poetry I have tried to show you the pain, suffering, misery, and regret that is death row by sharing with you a combination of the inmate's letters (in italics) and their poetry. It is difficult for us to imagine what it's like to exist on the row, but this book gives us a glimpse inside the minds of people who do know and want to keep others from making the same mistakes. I have not forgotten the victims, how could I, but my focus here is on the future & the hope of prevention through education. In order to break the cycle of violence in America we must first understand its causes. Once we know the reasons for violence we must each ask the question: "What can I do to prevent violence in my life?" I asked that question three years ago and this book is my reply.
What will your answer be?

                                            The editor.